Praise for Ashley Davis Prend's *Claim Your Inner Grown-up*:

"What an insightful... psychological, and spi... *Your Inner Grown-up* is a... and practical guide to emotional, sonal development. Her tou... ity! Ashley Davis Prend's *Claim* will lead readers to the deep s... for anyone interested in per- choosing transcendence over indulg... with a soft touch approach ...faction that comes from

—Dave Pelzer, au...

...f *A Man Named Dave*

"Mix a pinch of Dr. Laura's ethic of responsibilit,... a teaspoon of M. Scott Peck's compassion and an ounce of Gibran's spirituality, heat and serve Ashley Davis Prend's *Claim Your Inner Grown-up*. Your body, mind, and spirit will jump with joy (er . . . responsible joy)."

—Warren Farrell, Ph.D.,
author of *Why Men Are the Way They Are*

"Ashley Davis Prend's *Claim Your Inner Grown-up* is an indispensable guide to eliminating the shortage of real maturity among adults. Like any good teacher, she asks us to set our sights high, then provides us with the tools and instruction we need to achieve those goals. Ashley Davis Prend offers guidance and encouragement, but not doctrine or dogma. The practical, powerful exercises are especially helpful. I can't think of anyone who wouldn't benefit from this wise and warmhearted book."

—Harold Bloomfield, M.D.,
author of *Making Peace with Your Past*

"In this thought-provoking and inspirational book, the self-help movement itself finally comes of age. Both your life and the world we share will be the better for it."

—Forrest Church, author of *Lifecraft*

"What a wise book! It will bring blessings to many who read it."
—Rabbi Harold Kushner,
author of *When Bad Things Happen to Good People*

ASHLEY DAVIS PREND, A.C.S.W., is a psychotherapist and grief counselor, and the author of *Transcending Loss: Understanding the Lifelong Impact of Grief and How to Make it Meaningful*. She lives in New Hampshire with her husband and their three children.

DAVIS PREND

ALSO B*yrstanding the Lifelong Impact*

*Transcending Los*ow to Make It Meaningful

of Grief